HOLLY WEBB
Sticker and Activity Book
Kitten Fun

Find the answers on pages 23–2[?]

D1584753

STRIPES PUBLISHING
An imprint of Little Tiger Press
1 The Coda Centre, 189 Munster Road,
London SW6 6AW

First published in Great Britain in 2015

The activity on page 2 is taken from a previously
published title by Stripes Publishing, *My Secret Kitten*
The Story Kitten was first published by
Stripes Publishing in 2013 in *Moonlight Tales*
This abridged version first published in 2015

Text and puzzles copyright © Stripes Publishing, 2013, 2015
The Story Kitten copyright © Holly Webb, 2013, 2015
Inside illustrations copyright © Katherine Kirkland, 2013
and Artful Doodlers, 2014, 2015
Cover illustrations copyright © Sophy Williams, 2011
and Artful Doodlers, 2015
Sticker sheet illustrations copyright © Sophy Williams, 2008–2015,
Katherine Kirkland, 2013 and Artful Doodlers, 2015

ISBN: 978-1-84715-602-0

Printed and bound in China.

STP/1800/0053/0115

2 4 6 8 10 9 7 5 3 1

Stripes

My Cat Character

If you were a kitten, which breed would you be? This quiz will tell you!

1) My favourite food is...

a. Breakfast cereal – energy for when I'm out and about

b. Chocolate, and lots of it

c. Fruit and veg – good for my skin and hair

d. Fish and chips – brain food

2) My bedroom is...

a. A mess of trainers, balls, rackets and socks

b. My special sanctuary, so I keep it nice and neat

c. A pretty haven of beautiful clothes and gorgeous accessories

d. Lined with books and games

3) My favourite kind of film is...

a. Action

b. Comedy

c. Drama

d. Mystery

4) My clothes are...

a. Sleek, sporty and no frills

b. Perfect for lounging about at home

c. The latest trend

d. Smart but comfortable

5) My favourite time of year is...

a. Summer – a great time to get out and about

b. Winter – I love snuggling up in a warm, cosy room

c. Spring – time for a wardrobe refresh

d. Autumn – back to school to see my mates

6) My ideal birthday party would be...

a. A sports day in the park

b. A sleepover at my house with lots of friends

c. An afternoon out shopping

d. A day trip to a new place

Mostly As...
Spirited Siamese
You're energetic, always on the go, and you love playing sports and games with your friends.

Mostly Cs...
Pampered Persian
These cats are known for their good looks, and you're just as stylish!

Mostly Bs...
Mellow moggy
You're a real housecat – you love curling up with a good book and spending time with your family.

Mostly Ds...
Bright Russian Blue
Just like these cats, you're smart and curious, and you like to explore and find out new things.

Matching Moggies

The kittens below all have
matching shadows — except one. Can
you connect each kitten to its shadow,
then circle the odd cat out?

A

1

2

3

B

C

4

5

D

Help Fluff!

Poor Fluff is lost! Can you help her find her way home? Trace a path through the maze below, avoiding the bushes.

Crossword Cats

Look at the clues below and fill
in the crossword with these
favourite kitten things.

Top Tip!
Count the number of
spaces to see how
many letters will be in
the word.

Across

1. You'd better hope your cat
   doesn't catch one of these!

2. Cats use their tongues to
   l ___ themselves clean

3. An evening meal

4. A round toy that rolls along
   the floor

Down

5. Cats like to get tangled in
   w ___

6. Another word for a hug —
   kittens love these!

7. A short sleep

8. The sound a cat makes
   when it's happy

Purr-fect Puss

Jess loves to look her best! Colour her
in and then stick on some accessories to
make her feel extra special. You could add
a sparkly collar, bows or even a hat!

Done

Meow Mix-up!

The words below have got all muddled up! Can you unscramble the letters to find five kitten objects? Then look for the stickers that match the words.

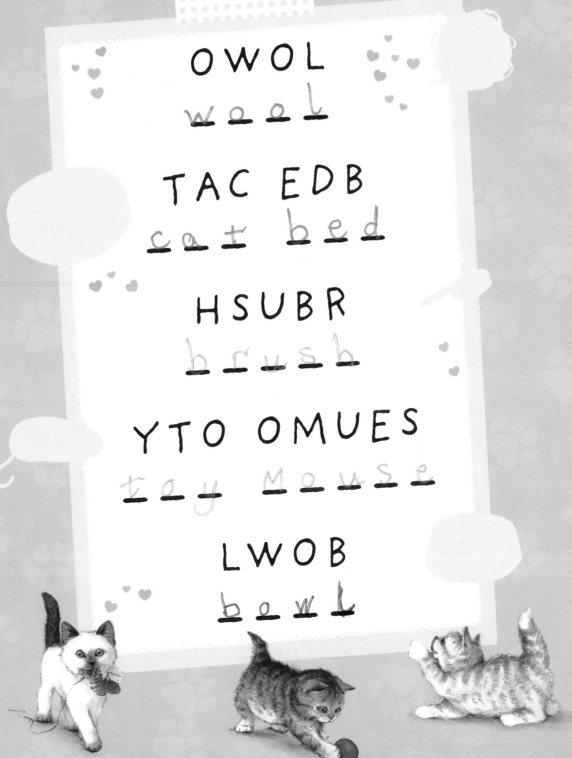

OWOL

wool

TAC EDB

cat bed

HSUBR

brush

YTO OMUES

toy mouse

LWOB

bowl

Hidden Kittens

There are eight breeds of cat hiding in this wordsearch. Can you find them all? The words may be across, down or diagonal.

Q	N	S	I	A	M	E	S	E	A	B	R
J	O	Q	A	A	Y	U	P	J	R	E	U
Y	B	E	N	G	A	L	H	A	A	F	S
P	S	S	W	O	S	K	Y	K	G	G	S
E	O	X	R	V	K	Y	N	E	D	K	I
R	G	T	A	B	B	Y	X	R	O	L	A
S	W	E	V	E	C	A	N	K	L	C	N
I	A	R	R	R	M	A	E	U	L	Y	B
A	N	A	X	M	M	Y	S	W	T	V	L
N	P	M	O	R	L	Y	S	G	Q	K	U
T	O	R	I	S	I	S	E	O	B	Y	E
J	P	B	L	O	C	L	L	N	F	V	T

TABBY   BENGAL

PERSIAN   RUSSIAN BLUE

BIRMAN   RAGDOLL

SIAMESE   SPHYNX

Dot to Dot

Can you join the dots to complete
the picture and find out what Milly is
playing with? Then draw or stick in
some other toys for her.

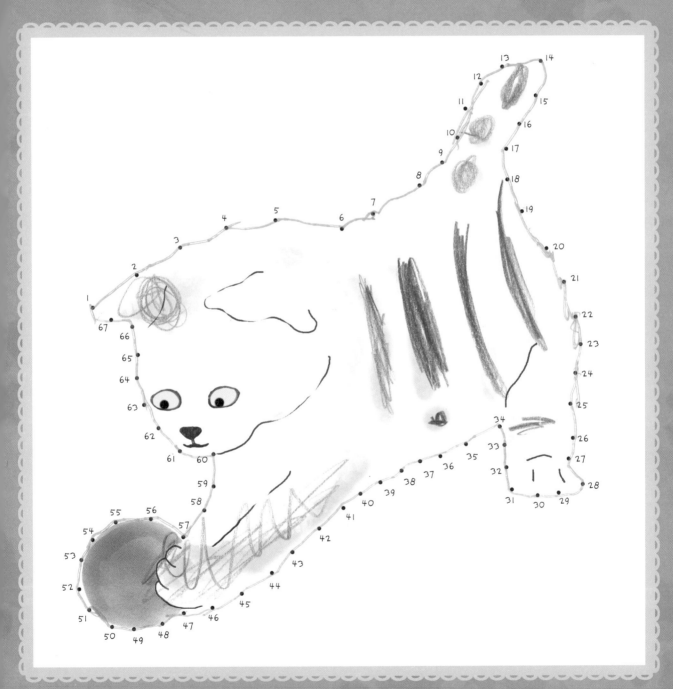

Cute Cats

Can you fill in the missing letters
below to finish the sentences and find
out what each of these cats are doing?

Bella likes climbing t r e e s.

Jack is s i t t i n g in the flowerpot.

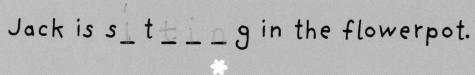

Molly is f e e d i n g her kittens.

Sky is playing with some f e a t h e r s

Spot the Difference

Lulu and Martha love cuddling their kitten! There are ten differences in the second picture. Can you spot them all?

What Next?

Look at the four patterns below.
Can you work out the next picture in
the sequence and find the matching
sticker at the back of this book?

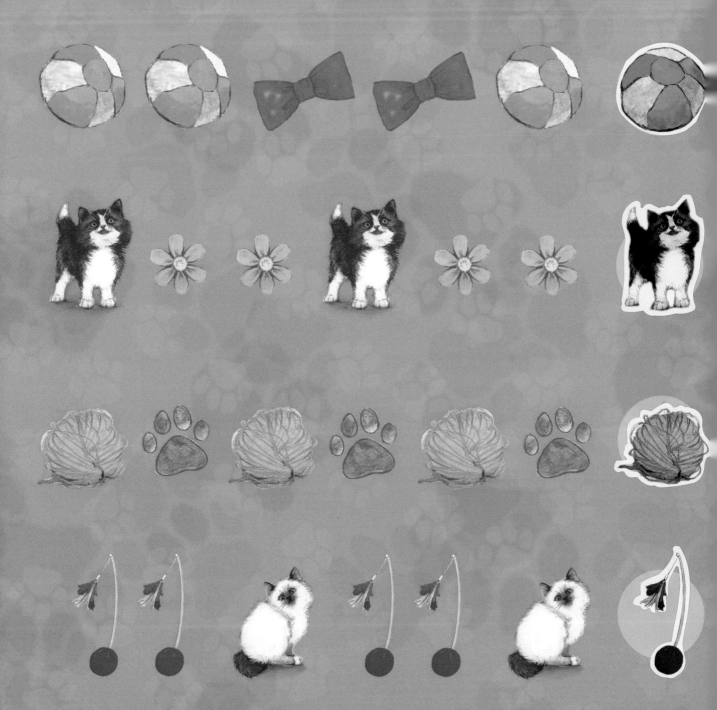

Cat Creation

Copy this kitten using the grid to help you. Once you've drawn your cat, why not colour him in and add some decorations using the stickers at the back of this book!

No Place Like Home

Kittens need a fun and safe place to play. Colour in this room and find some other things your cat might like on the sticker pages to make the perfect kitten space.

Odd Cat Out

Look carefully at the five sets of
pictures below. One picture in each row
is different to the others. Can you find it
and circle it?

Tangled Up!

It's play time! Follow the trails to find out which object matches with each kitten.

What's My Name?

There are ten popular kitten names in this wordsearch. Can you find them all? The words may be across, down or diagonal.

F	L	U	F	F	R	H	W	Q	A	A	W
J	O	Q	A	A	Y	O	A	J	D	Y	H
Y	A	V	C	I	N	B	U	R	U	T	I
P	O	P	P	Y	S	I	A	K	R	L	S
E	O	X	R	V	K	M	C	E	E	Y	K
R	G	C	A	B	B	Y	E	R	U	U	E
S	T	A	R	M	C	G	I	N	G	E	R
I	A	R	R	Y	X	K	E	T	K	Y	S
A	N	A	X	K	O	Y	E	W	T	V	S
N	P	M	O	L	L	J	B	H	Q	K	S
T	O	E	T	O	I	S	E	O	B	Y	K
J	P	L	L	S	C	L	M	I	L	L	Y

FLUFF	POPPY
WHISKERS	STAR
MILLY	CARAMEL
SKY	JET
GINGER	HARRY

Dream Kittens!

Draw some gorgeous cats in the frames below. You could even add sticker accessories to make the kittens look picture perfect!

The Story Kitten

By Holly Webb

"Tell me again," Lulu begged, clutching at Martha's pyjamas so that her big sister couldn't climb off her bed.

It was a freezing-cold night and the wind was whistling. Martha had looked out at the stars when she'd drawn the curtains. They hung in the sky, floating just beyond the branches of the old tree outside the window. Martha had thought she could reach out and pick a star, silver and sparkling, and make a wish on it.

"Go on!" Lulu prodded her.

"One day…" The story always started the same way. "One day, maybe even quite soon, we'll have a kitten of our very own."

"To keep," Lulu added. That was important.

"Yes, to keep."

"What will it look like?"

"It will be a black kitten. Black as night. But with a little white furry star under its chin and a long black tail, with just a tiny touch of white at the end."

"And we'll call him Sam," Lulu said. Both Lulu and Martha thought Sam was a gorgeous name for a cat.

"Will he sleep on my bed?" Lulu asked dreamily.

"Yes, most nights," her sister agreed. "Sometimes he'll sleep on my bed instead."

Lulu nodded. That was fair.

"Martha, how will we get the kitten?" Lulu asked.

Martha frowned. They hadn't thought about that before. Somehow, their beautiful black and white story kitten was too special to have come from a pet shop, like any ordinary cat.

"He'll find us," Martha decided. "On a moonlit night, full of stars, just like tonight. It will be so dark that no one will see him as he goes past. Except for the little white tip of his tail, so it will look like a tiny white star floating by."

"Will Sam be OK, travelling all on his own?" Lulu asked anxiously. "He's only a very little kitten."

"Yes, but he's an adventurer." Martha thought for a minute, and smiled. "He's been a witch's kitten, but all those spells made him sneeze, so he had to give that up. And then he was a ship's cat on a pirate ship."

"Did he ever get seasick?" Lulu murmured sleepily.

"Yes, a little bit, just like you. So now he wants to settle down and find a forever home in a house that doesn't sway up and down."

Lulu suddenly sat up in bed. "What colour are Sam's eyes?" she asked excitedly. "I've forgotten."

Martha knew that she hadn't really. The kitten's eyes were one of Lulu's favourite parts. "They're green," she reminded her sister. "A soft blue-green, like the sea. Maybe because he did some of his growing up on a pirate ship," she added.

"Perhaps he really is coming tonight…" Lulu suggested, her eyes shining. She pulled the duvet up to her chin and stared hopefully at Martha.

"I said a moonlit night, Lulu. That's all. A night *like* tonight. Not actually, really tonight."

"But it could be," Lulu said stubbornly. "It could be tonight. Couldn't it?"

"I suppose so," Martha sighed. She loved this story, too, but she had told Lulu about the kitten so many times now. She just wished it was true. Or that they could have any cat. She wouldn't mind if it wasn't their little black story kitten. She would love a tabby cat, or a ginger, as long as it was theirs.

Lulu prodded Martha again. "Where is he, Martha? Where's Sam now?"

"He'll be walking past the school. He might even take a shortcut through the playground and see your classroom. And then he'll slip through the railings and out on to the street. He'll be coming the same way that we walk home from school."

"Oh! He'll go past all my favourite places!" Lulu said excitedly. "Is he going to go past the swings?"

"Yes. He might go down the big slide. Or maybe the scramble net. That would remind him of the pirate ship, when he used to climb the rigging and sit in the crow's nest with the look-out. Then he'll be almost at our road."

Martha sighed silently. She could picture it. The little black kitten, stalking through the shadows, stopping here and there to pounce on a fallen leaf, or sniff at an interesting smell floating out from under a hedge.

"Is he nearly at our house?" Lulu asked.

"Yes." Martha nodded. "He's slipped down the alleyway, past the wheelie bins. The gate's locked, so he wriggled under the hedge."

"He's in the garden!" Lulu gasped. "But we don't have a cat flap – how's he going to get in?"

Martha eyed her worriedly. "It's only a story, Lulu, remember."

"I don't care! Tell me!"

"Ummm. He'll climb the tree," Martha said.

She nodded towards the window. It was still windy and the branches were tap-tapping against the glass.

"I can hear him!" Lulu stared wide-eyed at the window. "Mewing! Didn't you hear, Martha?"

"That's the wind. Sam's just a story, Lulu. One day we'll have our own cat, but this one's just a story kitten."

"It was him," Lulu said stubbornly. She pushed back the duvet and climbed out of bed. "You'll see."

Martha sighed, and followed her little sister to the window. Lulu was hesitating, her fingers on the curtains. She wanted to believe so much – she didn't want to see just the darkness, and the tree…

Martha put her arm round Lulu's shoulders and drew the curtains open. "You see," she said. "I'm really sorry, Lu." The wind mewed, louder and louder, and Martha shivered.

But Lulu had frozen. "Look," she whispered. "It's him. Just like you said."

Martha looked out of the window, her heart thumping so hard she felt dizzy.

Balanced on the spindly branch was a small black kitten, with a white-tipped tail, mewing loudly, as if to tell them to hurry up and let him in.

Blinking, Martha turned the key and pushed the window open. The kitten jumped on to the sill. He rubbed his head against Lulu's cheek and peered mischievously up at Martha.

"Just like you said, Martha," Lulu whispered, as she gently wrapped her arms round the little black kitten. "You came all that way, Sam."

"I wished," Martha murmured. "I wished, and he came."

Answers

ge 3

is the odd one out (IC, 2D, 4A, 5B)

ge 4

is is the route home:

ge 5

our crossword should look

ke this:

```
  W
M O U S E
  O           P
  L I C K     U
    U         R
    D I N N E R
    D     A
B A L L   P
    E
```

Page 7

The words are: WOOL, CAT BED, BRUSH, TOY MOUSE, BOWL

Page 8

Your wordsearch should look like this:

Page 9

Milly is playing with a ball

Page 10

The words are: trees, sitting, feeding, feathers

23

Answers

Page 11

The differences in picture two are circled below:

Page 12

Your patterns should look like this:

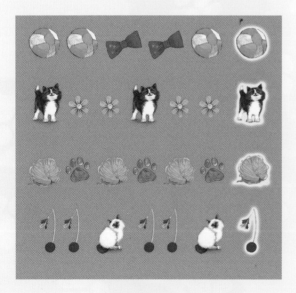

Page 15

Row 1: The fifth kitten has a patch missing

Row 2: The first kitten has a black tail

Row 3: The second kitten has open eyes

Row 4: The fourth kitten has different feathers

Row 5: The third kitten is facing t opposite way

Page 16

1B, 2C, 3A

Page 17

Your wordsearch should look like this: